VIDEO GUIDE and TRAINING WORKBOOK for the *Early Childhood Environment Rating Scale* *Revised Edition*

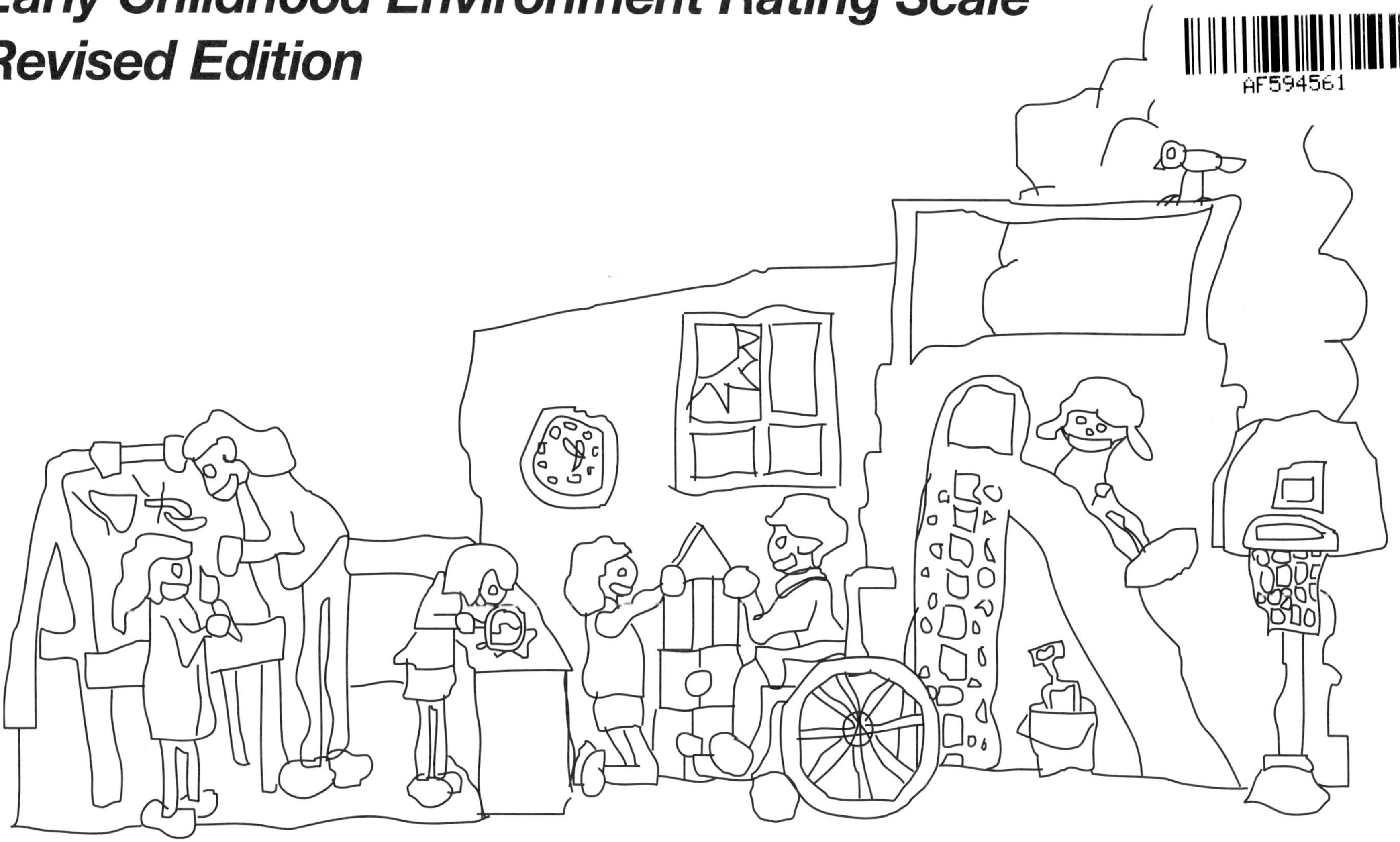

Thelma Harms and Debby Cryer
Frank Porter Graham Child Development Center
University of North Carolina at Chapel Hill

Official training materials for the *Early Childhood Environment Rating Scale–Revised Edition,* by Thelma Harms, Richard M. Clifford, and Debby Cryer

Contents

PART I: PREPARATION FOR ACCURATE SCORING ***1***

A. The 43 Items the ECERS-R 1

B. Sample Item and Scoresheet 2

C. Instructions for Using the ECERS-R 3

D. Scrambled Item Activities 5

E. Sample Situations for Scoring Practice 6

PART II: ITEMS FOR SCORING THE VIDEO OBSERVATIONS ***9***

PART III: OPTIONAL ACTIVITIES ***18***

A. Asking Questions 18

B. Follow-Up Practice Observation 18

Form for Calculating ECERS–R Interrater Reliability 19

For use with the ECERS-R training video (now available in both VHS and DVD), *Video Observations for the Early Childhood Environment Rating Scale-Revised Edition,* written by Thelma Harms and Debby Cryer, produced by Julie Dixon of word and pictures, inc. Development of this package was partially funded by the A. L. Mailman Family Foundation and the Smith Richardson Foundation.

Both *Early Childhood Environment Rating Scale-Revised Edition,* by Thelma Harms, Richard M. Clifford, and Debby Cryer (ISBN 0-8077-3751-8), and *Video Observations for the Early Childhood Environment Rating Scale-Revised Edition,* by Thelma Harms and Debby Cryer (ISBN 0-8077-3834-4), are available from Teachers College Press.

Cover design by Turner McCollum

Published by Teachers College Press, 1234 Amsterdam Avenue, New York, NY 10027

ISBN-13: 978-0-8077-3835-1 ISBN-10: 0-8077-3835-2

Printed on acid-free paper

Manufactured in the United States of America

23 22 21 20 19 18 17 16

* * * * * * * * * * * * * * * * Read This Before Starting Videotape * * * * * * * * * * * * * * * *

Organization of the Video Guide

Part I of this guide includes print activities to prepare you to use the ECERS–R accurately. It is essential to complete all the preparation activities in Part I before viewing any of the video observations on the videotape. Part II includes the ECERS–R items and Notes for Clarification for use in scoring the video observations. Part III includes optional activities for further training.

Periodically, the videotape will instruct you to stop the tape and complete an activity.
When the tape instructs you to "Stop: Complete Part I of Your Video Guide" turn to page 1 in this guide. All other "Stop" activities will be found in Part II of the Guide, beginning on page 9.

* * * * * * * * * * * * * * * * * * Now Start the Videotape * * * * * * * * * * * * * * * * * *

PART I: PREPARATION FOR ACCURATE SCORING

A. Review the 43 items in the 7 subscales of the ECERS-R listed below, as an introduction to the range of items included in the scale.

Space and Furnishings
1. Indoor space
2. Furniture for routine care, play and learning
3. Furnishings for relaxation and comfort
4. Room arrangement for play
5. Space for privacy
6. Child-related display
7. Space for gross motor play
8. Gross motor equipment

Personal Care Routines
9. Greeting/departing
10. Meals/snacks
11. Nap/rest
12. Toileting/diapering
13. Health practices
14. Safety practices

Language-Reasoning
15. Books and pictures
16. Encouraging children to communicate
17. Using language to develop reasoning skills
18. Informal use of language

Activities
19. Fine motor
20. Art
21. Music/movement
22. Blocks
23. Sand/watcr
24. Dramatic play
25. Nature/science
26. Math/number
27. Use of TV, video, and/or computers
28. Promoting acceptance of diversity

Interaction
29. Supervision of gross motor activities
30. General supervision of children (other than gross motor)
31. Discipline
32. Staff-child interactions
33. Interactions among children

Program Structure
34. Schedule
35. Free play
36. Group time
37. Provisions for children with disabilities

Parents and Staff
38. Provisions for parents
39. Provisions for personal needs of staff
40. Provisions for professional needs of staff
41. Staff interaction and cooperation
42. Supervision and evaluation of staff
43. Opportunities for professional growth

B. Review the Sample Item and Its Scoresheet Section

Inadequate 1	2	Minimal 3	4	Good 5	6	Excellent 7

4. Room arrangement for play

Inadequate 1	Minimal 3	Good 5	Excellent 7
1.1 No interest centers* defined. 1.2 Visual supervision of play area is difficult.	3.1 At least two interest centers defined. 3.2 Visual supervision of play area is not difficult. 3.3 Sufficient space for several activities to go on at once (Ex. floor space for blocks, table space for manipulatives, easel for art). 3.4 Most spaces for play are accessible to children with disabilities enrolled in the group. *NA permitted.*	5.1 At least three interest centers defined and conveniently equipped (Ex. water provided near art area; shelving adequate for blocks and manipulatives). 5.2 Quiet and active centers placed to not interfere with one another (Ex. reading or listening area separated from blocks or housekeeping). 5.3 Space is arranged so most activities are not interrupted (Ex. shelves placed so children walk around, not through, activities; placement of furniture discourages rough play or running).	7.1 At least five different interest centers provide a variety of learning experiences. 7.2 Centers are organized for independent use by children (Ex. labeled open shelves; labeled containers for toys; open shelves are not overcrowded; play space near toy storage). 7.3 Additional materials available to add to or change centers.

Note for Clarification

* An interest center is an area where materials, organized by type, are stored so that they are accessible to children, and appropriately furnished play space is provided for children to participate in a particular kind of play. Examples of interest centers are art activities, blocks, dramatic play, reading, nature/science, and manipulatives/fine motor.

Question

(7.3) Are there any additional materials available that you add to the interest centers?

4. Room arrangement 1 2 3 4 5 6 7

	Y	N		Y	N	NA		Y	N		Y	N
1.1	☐	☐	3.1	☐	☐		5.1	☐	☐	7.1	☐	☐
1.2	☐	☐	3.2	☐	☐		5.2	☐	☐	7.2	☐	☐
			3.3	☐	☐		5.3	☐	☐	7.3	☐	☐
			3.4	☐	☐	☐						

C. Read the Instructions for Using the ECERS-R

Scoring System

1. Read the entire scale carefully, including the Items, Notes for Clarification, and Questions. In order to be accurate, all ratings have to be based as exactly as possible on the indicators provided in the scale items.
2. The scale should be kept readily available and consulted frequently during the entire observation to make sure that the scores are assigned accurately.
3. Examples that differ from those given in the indicators but seem comparable may be used as a basis for giving credit for an indicator.
4. Scores should be based on the current situation that is observed or reported by staff, not on future plans. In the absence of observable information on which to base your rating, you may use answers given by the staff during the question period to assign scores.
5. When scoring an item, always start reading from 1 (inadequate) and progress upward till the correct score is reached.
6. Ratings are to be assigned in the following way:
   - A rating of 1 must be given if *any* indicator under 1 is scored Yes.
   - A rating of 2 is given when all indicators under 1 are scored No and at least half of the indicators under 3 are scored Yes.
   - A rating of 3 is given when all indicators under 1 are scored No and all indicators under 3 are scored Yes.
   - A rating of 4 is given when all indicators under 3 are met and at least half of the indicators under 5 are scored Yes.
   - A rating of 5 is given when all indicators under 5 are scored Yes.
   - A rating of 6 is given when all indicators under 5 are met and at least half of the indicators under 7 are scored Yes.
   - A rating of 7 is given when all indicators under 7 are scored Yes.
   - A score of NA (Not Applicable) may only be given for indicators or for entire items when "NA permitted" is shown on the scale and on the Score Sheet. Indicators that are scored NA are not counted when determining the rating for an item, and items scored NA are not counted when calculating subscale and total scale scores.
7. To calculate average subscale scores, sum the scores for each item in the subscale and divide by the number of items scored. The total mean scale score is the sum of all item scores for the entire scale divided by the number of items scored.

Explanations of Terms Used Throughout the Scale

1. **Accessible** means children can reach and use materials, furnishings, equipment, and so forth. This does not mean that every child has to have access at all times. For example, access may be limited to a certain number of children in an area or limited to certain times of the day.
2. **A substantial portion of the day** means at least one third of the time the children are in attendance. For example, 1 hour out of a 3-hour program, or 3 hours out of a 9-hour program.
3. In order to differentiate the meaning of the words **"some"** and **"many"** the materials in several items are separated into categories in the Notes for Clarification. For example, gross motor equipment is separated into *stationary equipment* and *portable equipment;* fine motor materials are separated into *small building toys, art materials, manipulatives,* and *puzzles;* nature/science includes categories of materials such as *collections of natural objects, living things, nature science books, games,* or *toys,* and *nature/science activities* such as cooking and simple experiments.
4. **Staff** generally refers to the adults who are directly involved with the children, the teaching staff. In the scale, staff is used in the plural because there is usually more than one staff member working with a group. When individual staff members handle things differently, it is necessary to arrive at a score that characterizes the overall impact on the children of all the staff members. For example, in a room when one staff member is very verbal and the other is relatively nonverbal, the score is determined by how well the children's needs for verbal input are being met.

Administration of the Scale

1. The scale is designed to be used with one room or one group at a time, for children 2½ through 5 years of age. A block of at least 2 hours should be set aside for observation and rating if you are an outside observer.
2. Before you begin your observation, complete as much as possible of the identifying information on the top of the first page of the Score Sheet. You may need to ask the teacher for some of the information. By the end of the observation, make sure all the identifying information requested on the first page is complete.
3. Take a few minutes at the beginning of your observation to orient yourself to the classroom.
   - You may want to start with Items 1-6 in Space and Furnishings because they are easy to observe.
   - Some items require observation of events and activities that occur only at specific times of the day (i.e., Items 9-12 in Personal Care Routines, Items 7, 8, and 29 covering gross motor play). Be aware of those items so that you can observe and rate them as they occur.
   - Score items that assess interactions only after you have observed for a sufficient time to get a representative picture (i.e., Items 30-33 in Interactions; 34-37 in Program Structure; 41 in Parents and Staff).
   - Items 19-28 in Activities will require both inspection of materials and observation of use of materials.
4. Be careful not to disrupt the ongoing activities while you are observing.
   - Maintain a pleasant but neutral facial expression.
   - Do not interact with the children unless you see something dangerous that must be handled immediately.
   - Do not talk to or interrupt the staff.
5. You need to arrange a time with the teacher to ask questions about indicators you were not able to observe. The teacher should be free of responsibility for children when he or she is answering questions. Approximately 20 minutes will be required for questions. In order to make best use of the time set aside for asking questions:
   - Use the sample questions provided, whenever applicable.
   - If you have to ask questions about items for which no sample questions have been provided, jot your questions down on the Score Sheet or another Sheet of paper before talking with the teacher.
   - Ask only those questions needed to decide whether a higher score is possible.
   - Ask questions on one item at a time and take notes or decide on a score before you move on to the next item.

D. Complete the following Scrambled Item Activities

For the ECERS-R items that follow, the indicators for each level of quality are out of order. Read each of these Scrambled Items carefully. For each item, decide which description is Inadequate (1), Minimal (3), Good (5), and Excellent (7). Remember, for a rating of 7, all of 5 must be present, plus all of 7. The answer key for the Scrambled Items is in the Instructor's Guide.

22. Blocks

(a) _____

- At least two types of blocks and a variety of accessories accessible daily (Ex. large and small; homemade and commercial).
- Blocks and accessories are stored on open, labeled shelves (Ex. labeled with picture or outline of blocks).
- Some block play available outdoors.

(b) _____

- Enough blocks and accessories are accessible for at least two children to build independent structures at the same time.
- Some clear floor space used for block play.
- Blocks and accessories accessible for daily use

(c) _____

- Few blocks are accessible for children's play.

(d) _____

- Enough blocks and accessories are accessible for three or more children to build at the same time.
- Blocks and accessories are organized according to type.
- Special block area set aside out of traffic, with storage and suitable building surface (Ex. flat rug or other steady surface).
- Block area accessible for play for a substantial portion of the day.

Notes for Clarification

Blocks are materials suitable for building sizable structures. Types of blocks are ***unit blocks*** (wooden or plastic, including shapes such as rectangles, squares, triangles, and cylinders); ***large hollow blocks*** (wooden, plastic, or cardboard); ***homemade blocks*** (materials such as food boxes and plastic containers). Note that small blocks, including interlocking blocks such as Lego, are considered under Fine Motor, Item 19.

–Accessories enrich block play. Examples are toy people, animals, vehicles, and road signs.

18. Informal use of language*

(a) _____

- Many staff-child conversations during free play and routines.
- Language is primarily used by staff to exchange information with children and for social interaction.
- Staff add information to expand on ideas presented by children.
- Staff encourage communication among children, including those with disabilities (Ex. remind children to listen to one another; teach all children to sign if classmate uses sign language).

(b) _____

- Some staff-child conversation (Ex. ask "yes/no" or short answer questions; give short answers to children's questions).
- Children allowed to talk much of the day.

(c) _____

- Staff have individual conversations with most of the children.
- Children are asked questions to encourage them to give longer and more complex answers. (Ex. young child is asked "what" or "where" questions; older child is asked "why" or "how" questions).

(d) _____

- Staff talk to children primarily to control their behavior and manage routines.
- Staff rarely respond to children's talk.
- Children's talk is discouraged much of the day.

Notes for Clarification

–When multiple staff are working with the children, base the score for this item on the overall impact of the staff's communication with the children. The intent of this item is that children's need for language stimulation is met.

–In order to be given credit for "conversation," there should be some mutual listening and talking/responding from both the staff and child. This is different from one-way communication such as giving directions or commands. For children with less verbal ability, the response may not be in words but may involve gestures, sign language, or communication devices.

–Expand means staff respond verbally to add more information to what a child says. For example, a child says, "Look at this truck," and the teacher responds, "It's a red dump truck. See, it has a place to carry things."

–To give credit for these indicators several instances must be observed.

E. Complete the Following Sample Situations for Scoring Practice

Read the descriptions of the following situations, which are similar to ones you might observe in an early childhood program. Using the specified ECERS-R item with the Notes for Clarification, score the sample situation. Write your reason for scoring the way you did. Record your score for each indicator as well as the overall quality score. The answer key to the Sample Situations is in the Instructor's Guide.

Use Item 2 to score this sample situation:

You are observing a group of 4- and 5-year-olds, none of whom have identified disabilities. During the morning you see children taking materials from the many open shelves in various areas of the room and finding space on nearby tables and rugs to play with them. They also go to their cubbies occasionally to put artwork away or to get things they have brought from home. The furniture in the room seems new, and all of it is sturdy. During snack, all the children and teachers sit down together at the tables. The rest of the time the furniture is used for play. You notice that less than half of the children are big enough so that their feet rest on the floor when they sit on the chairs, so some of them kneel on the chairs to reach the table.

There is a woodworking bench in the corner with scraps of wood stored in a box on a shelf under the table. The cots are stored in a corner of the room, out of the way, but easily accessible. They have clean sheets on them, and each cot has a child's name on it.

Inadequate 1	2	Minimal 3	4	Good 5	6	Excellent 7

2. Furniture for routine care, play, and learning*

1.1 Insufficient basic furniture for routine care, play, and learning (Ex. not enough chairs for all children to use at the same time; very few open shelves for toys).

1.2 Furniture is generally in such poor repair that children could be injured (Ex. splinters or exposed nails, wobbly legs on chairs).

3.1 Sufficient furniture for routine care, play, and learning.

3.2 Most furniture is sturdy and in good repair.

3.3 Children with disabilities† have the adaptive furniture they need (Ex. adaptive chairs or bolsters are available for children with physical disabilities).
NA permitted.

5.1 Most furniture is child-sized.‡

5.2 All furniture is sturdy and in good repair.

5.3 Adaptive furniture permits inclusion of children with disabilities† with peers (Ex. child using special chair can sit at table with others).
NA permitted.

7.1 Routine care furniture is convenient to use (Ex. cots/mats stored for easy access).

7.2 Woodwork bench, sand/water table, or easel used.

Notes for Clarification

* Basic furniture: tables and chairs used for meals/snacks and activities; mats or cots for rest or nap; cubbies or other storage for children's things; low open shelves for play/learning materials. To be given credit for low open shelves, they must be used for toys and materials that children can reach by themselves.

† If there are no children with disabilities enrolled or if children with disabilities do not need adaptive furniture, mark NA for 3.3 and 5.3.

‡ Since children are different sizes at different ages, the intent here is that furniture should be the right size for the children in care. Furniture that is smaller than adult-sized may be the right size for a 6- or 7-year-old, but not small enough for a 2- or 3-year-old. For chairs to be considered child-sized, the children's feet must rest on the floor when seated. Table height should allow children's knees to fit under the table and elbows to be above the table.

2. Furniture for care, play, and learning — 1 2 3 4 5 6 7

	Y	N		Y	N	NA		Y	N	NA		Y	N
1.1	☐	☐	3.1	☐	☐		5.1	☐	☐		7.1	☐	☐
1.2	☐	☐	3.2	☐	☐		5.2	☐	☐		7.2	☐	☐
			3.3	☐	☐	☐	5.3	☐	☐	☐			

Use Item 28 to score this sample situation:

You are observing in a multiage classroom where the children are 3 to 5 years of age, and most, but not all of them, are African American. The bulletin boards are decorated in honor of Black History month with large figures representing African tribes. There are many pictures of famous Black Americans on the walls. There are also some interracial group pictures. The dramatic play props that represent different cultures include the dolls of several races and plastic foods representing different cultures, dress-ups that include men's and women's clothes, as well as some clothes and cooking utensils associated with different countries. Both boys and girls use all of these props freely.

Some books have pretend animals as main characters, but you find many books, pictures, puzzles, and toy people showing people of different cultures, races, ages and abilities. The pictures and stories all portray the characters positively. As you look at the many pictures around the room and in books, you see that both males and females are shown doing many tasks, such as housekeeping, parenting, or as firefighters, sports figures, truck drivers, and doctors.

At music time the children sing an African song and a Native American song as well as some preschool favorites. There are many music tapes from a variety of cultures near the tape player. The teacher says she plays quiet classical music at naptime, too. You see that the teachers handle the children evenly, showing no prejudice. You ask the teacher if there are ever any problems with prejudice among the children or others in the class, and she says, "Luckily, we have never had problems like that." You ask if activities are ever done to help children understand and accept cultural differences in our society, and she tells you that in cooking activities, she tries to use recipes that are associated with different cultures, and that at holiday times, all holidays are talked about.

Inadequate		Minimal		Good		Excellent
1	2	3	4	5	6	7

28. Promoting acceptance of diversity

1.1 No racial or cultural diversity visible in materials* (Ex. all toys and pictures are of one race, all print materials are about one culture, all print and audio materials are in one language where bilingualism is prevalent).

1.2 Materials present only stereotypes of races, cultures, ages, abilities, and gender.

1.3 Staff demonstrate prejudice against others (Ex. against child or other adult from difference race or cultural group, against person with disability).

3.1 Some racial and cultural diversity visible in materials (Ex. multi-racial or multi-cultural dolls, books, or bulletin board pictures, music tapes from many cultures; in bilingual areas some materials accessible in children's primary language).

3.2 Materials show diversity (Ex. different races, cultures, ages, abilities, or gender) in a positive way.

3.3 Staff intervene appropriately to counteract prejudice shown by children or other adults (Ex. discuss similarities and differences; establish rules for fair treatment of others), *or* no prejudice is shown.

5.1 Many books, pictures and materials accessible showing people of different races, cultures, ages, abilities, and gender in non-stereotyping roles (Ex. both historical and current images; males and females shown doing many different types of work including traditional and non-traditional roles).

5.2 Some props representing various cultures included for use in dramatic play (Ex. dolls of different races, ethnic clothing, cooking and eating utensils from various cultural groups).

7.1 Inclusion of diversity is part of daily routines and play activities (Ex. ethnic foods are a regular part of meals/snacks; music tapes and songs from different cultures included at music time).

7.2 Activities included to promote understanding and acceptance of diversity (Ex. parents encouraged to share family customs with children; many cultures represented in holiday celebration).

Note for Clarification

* When assessing diversity in materials, consider all areas and materials used by children, including pictures and photos displayed, books, puzzles, games, dolls, play people in the block area, puppets, music tapes, videos, and computer software.

28. Promoting acceptance of diversity 1 2 3 4 5 6 7

	Y	N		Y	N		Y	N		Y	N
1.1	☐	☐	3.1	☐	☐	5.1	☐	☐	7.1	☐	☐
1.2	☐	☐	3.2	☐	☐	5.2	☐	☐	7.2	☐	☐
1.3	☐	☐	3.3	☐	☐						

Use Item 18 to score this sample situation:

You are observing in a classroom of 3-year-olds that has two teachers. Both seem to talk to the children a lot. You often hear them telling children what they need to do: "Sit down." "No running indoors." "Use the paints on the paper, not on the table." "It's time to clean up. Let's clean up so we will be able to go outside." Children tend to be quiet in the room and do not talk much. When their conversation becomes loud in the housekeeping center, one teacher tells them, "Keep the noise down, or you will have to leave the center."

You do notice a few conversations that happen between a teacher and a child. One child showed the teacher her new shoes, and the teacher said how pretty they were, and asked if she got the new shoes when she went shopping with her mom. But there are not many conversations like this in the 3 hours you spend in the classroom. At lunch time, the teachers quiz the children about the names of the foods they are eating, but otherwise tell the children to eat at lunch and not to talk.

Inadequate		Minimal		Good		Excellent
1	2	3	4	5	6	7

18. Informal use of language*

1.1 Staff talk to children primarily to control their behavior and manage routines.

1.2 Staff rarely respond to children's talk.

1.3 Children's talk is discouraged much of the day.

3.1 Some staff-child conversation† (Ex. ask "yes/no" or short answer questions; give short answers to children's questions).

3.2 Children allowed to talk much of the day.

5.1 Many staff-child conversations during free play and routines.

5.2 Language is primarily used by staff to exchange information with children and for social interaction.

5.3 Staff add information to expand‡ on ideas presented by children.**

5.4 Staff encourage communication among children, including those with disabilities (Ex. remind children to listen to one another; teach all children to sign if classmate uses sign language).

7.1 Staff have individual conversations with most of the children.**

7.2 Children are asked questions to encourage them to give longer and more complex answers.** (Ex. young child is asked "what" or "where" questions; older child is asked "why" or "how" questions).

Notes for Clarification

* When multiple staff are working with the children, base the score for this item on the overall impact of the staff's communication with the children. The intent of this item is that children's need for language stimulation is met.

† In order to be given credit for "conversation," there should be some mutual listening and talking/responding from both the staff and child. This is different from one-way communication such as giving directions or commands. For children with less verbal ability, the response may not be in words but may involve gestures, sign language, or communication devices.

‡ Expand means staff respond verbally to add more information to what a child says. For example, a child says, "Look at this truck," and the teacher responds, "It's a red dump truck. See, it has a place to carry things."

** To give credit for these indicators several instances must be observed.

18. Informal use of language 1 2 3 4 5 6 7

	Y	N		Y	N		Y	N		Y	N
1.1	☐	☐	3.1	☐	☐	5.1	☐	☐	7.1	☐	☐
1.2	☐	☐	3.2	☐	☐	5.2	☐	☐	7.2	☐	☐
1.3	☐	☐				5.3	☐	☐			
						5.4	☐	☐			

PART II: ITEMS FOR SCORING THE VIDEO OBSERVATIONS

Please note: In scoring the video observations, assume that what you see is typical of what goes on during the entire day.

Before restarting the videotape, read Item 6 - Child-related display

Inadequate 1	2	Minimal 3	4	Good 5	6	Excellent 7

6. Child-related display

Inadequate (1)	Minimal (3)	Good (5)	Excellent (7)
1.1 No materials displayed for children. 1.2 Inappropriate materials for predominant age group (Ex. materials in preschool classroom designed for older school-aged children or adults; pictures showing violence).	3.1 Appropriate* materials for predominant age group (Ex. photos of children; nursery rhymes; beginning reading and math for older preschoolers and kindergartners; seasonal displays). 3.2 Some children's work displayed.	5.1 Much of the display relates closely to current activities and children in group (Ex. artwork or photos about recent activities).† 5.2 Most of the display is work done by the children. 5.3 Many items displayed on child's eye level.	7.1 Individualized children's work predominates.‡ 7.2 Three-dimensional child-created work (Ex. playdough, clay, carpentry) displayed as well as flat work.

Notes for Clarification

* Appropriate means suitable for the developmental level of the age group and the individual abilities of the children. This concept is also referred to as developmentally appropriate and is used in a number of items in the scale.

† Recently completed artwork that does not relate to other things going on in the room does not count for this indicator.

‡ Individualized work means that each child has selected the subject and/or media and has carried out the work in his or her own creative way. Thus, individualized products look quite different from one another. Projects where children follow a teacher's example and little creativity is allowed are not considered individualized work.

* Restart tape *

Stop to score Item 6 - Child-related display

6. Child-related display	1 2 3 4 5 6 7		
Y N	Y N	Y N	Y N
1.1 ☐ ☐	3.1 ☐ ☐	5.1 ☐ ☐	7.1 ☐ ☐
1.2 ☐ ☐	3.2 ☐ ☐	5.2 ☐ ☐	7.2 ☐ ☐
		5.3 ☐ ☐	

* Restart tape *

Stop to read Item Item 24 - Dramatic play

Inadequate		Minimal		Good		Excellent
1	2	3	4	5	6	7

24. Dramatic play*

Inadequate (1)

1.1 No materials or equipment accessible for dress up or dramatic play.

Minimal (3)

3.1 Some dramatic play materials and furniture accessible, so children can act out family roles themselves (Ex. dress-up clothes, housekeeping props, dolls).

3.2 Materials are accessible for at least 1 hour daily.

3.3 Separate storage for dramatic play materials.

Good (5)

5.1 Many dramatic play materials accessible, including dress-up clothes.†

5.2 Materials accessible for a substantial portion of the day.

5.3 Props for at least two different themes accessible daily (Ex. housekeeping and work).

5.4 Dramatic play area clearly defined, with space to play and organized storage.

Excellent (7)

7.1 Materials rotated for a variety of themes (Ex. prop boxes for work, fantasy, and leisure themes).

7.2 Props provided to represent diversity (Ex. props representing various cultures; equipment used by people with disabilities).

7.3 Props provided for active dramatic play outdoors.‡

7.4 Pictures, stories, and trips used to enrich dramatic play.

Notes for Clarification

* Dramatic play is pretending or making believe. This type of play occurs when children act out roles themselves and when they manipulate figures such as small toy people in a doll house. Dramatic play is enhanced by props that encourage a variety of themes including ***housekeeping*** (Ex. dolls, child-sized furniture, dress-up, kitchen utensils); ***different kinds of work*** (Ex. office, construction, farm, store, fire fighting, transportation); ***fantasy*** (Ex. animals, dinosaurs, storybook characters); and ***leisure*** (Ex. camping, sports).

† Dress-up clothes should include more than the high-heeled shoes, dresses, purses, and women's hats commonly found in a playhouse area. Clothing worn by both men and women at work such as hardhats, transportation worker caps, and cowboy hats, as well as running shoes, clip-on ties, and jackets should be included.

‡ The intent of this indicator is that children are provided a large enough space so that their dramatic play can be very active and noisy without disrupting other activities. A large indoor space such as a gymnasium or multi-purpose room may be substituted for the outdoor space. Structures (such as small houses, cars, or boats) and props for camping, cooking, work, transportation, or dress-up clothes may be available to the children.

* Restart tape *

Stop to score Item 24 - Dramatic play

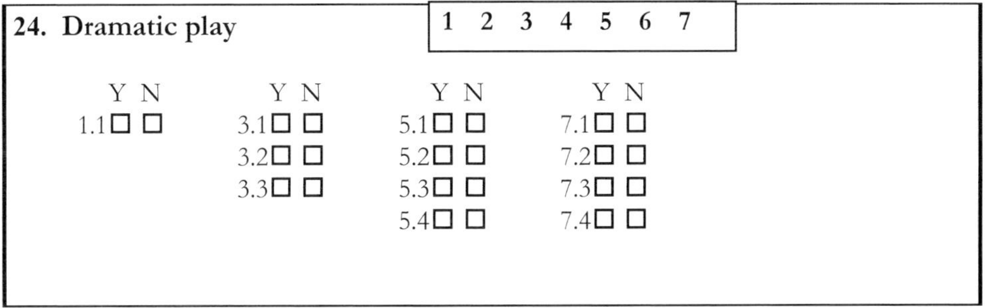

24. Dramatic play 1 2 3 4 5 6 7

Y N	Y N	Y N	Y N
1.1☐ ☐	3.1☐ ☐	5.1☐ ☐	7.1☐ ☐
	3.2☐ ☐	5.2☐ ☐	7.2☐ ☐
	3.3☐ ☐	5.3☐ ☐	7.3☐ ☐
		5.4☐ ☐	7.4☐ ☐

* Restart tape *

Stop to read Item 10 - Meals/snacks

	Inadequate		Minimal		Good		Excellent
	1	2	3	4	5	6	7
10. Meals/snacks	1.1 Meal/snack schedule is inappropriate (Ex. child is made to wait even if hungry). 1.2 Food served is of unacceptable nutritional value.* 1.3 Sanitary conditions not usually maintained (Ex. most children and/ or adults do not wash hands before handling food; tables not sanitized; toileting/diapering and food prepara tion areas not separated). 1.4 Negative social atmosphere (Ex. staff enforce manners harshly; force child to eat; chaotic atmosphere). 1.5 No accommodations made for children's food allergies. *NA permitted.*		3.1 Schedule appropriate for children. 3.2 Well-balanced meals/snacks.* 3.3 Sanitary conditions usually maintained.† 3.4 Nonpunitive atmosphere during meals/snacks. 3.5 Allergies posted and food/ beverage substitutions made. *NA permitted.* 3.6 Children with disabilities included at table with peers. *NA permitted.*		5.1 Most staff sit with children during meals and group snacks.‡ 5.2 Pleasant social atmosphere. 5.3 Children are encouraged to eat independently (Ex. child-sized *eating* utensils provided; special spoon or cup for child with disabilities). 5.4 Dietary restrictions of families followed. *NA permitted.*		7.1 Children help during meals/ snacks (Ex. set table, serve themselves, clear table, wipe up spills). 7.2 Child-sized *serving* utensils used by children to make self-help easier (Ex. children use small pitcher, sturdy serving bowls and spoons). 7.3 Meals and snacks are times for conversation (Ex. staff encourage children to talk about events of day and talk about things children are interested in; children talk with one another).

Notes for Clarification

* To determine nutritional adequacy, refer to nutrition guidelines for early childhood programs, such as USDA or Canadian guidelines. Check menu for the week in addition to observing food served. An occasional instance of not meeting the guidelines—for example, cupcakes for a birthday party instead of the scheduled snack—should not affect the rating. If no menu is available, ask the teacher to describe meals/snacks served for the past week.

† If sanitary conditions are usually maintained and if handwashing and other sanitary procedures are clearly a part of the program, credit can be given for 3.3 even if there is an occasional lapse in practice.

‡ Although staff may need to leave the table to assist with the meal, most of the time should be spent sitting with the children. It is not required that each table have a staff member. Some staff may help with serving, while others sit with children.

* Restart tape *

Stop to score Item 10 - Meals/snacks

10. Meals/snacks 1 2 3 4 5 6 7

	Y	N		Y	N	NA		Y	N	NA		Y	N
1.1	☐	☐	3.1	☐	☐		5.1	☐	☐		7.1	☐	☐
1.2	☐	☐	3.2	☐	☐		5.2	☐	☐		7.2	☐	☐
1.3	☐	☐	3.3	☐	☐		5.2	☐	☐		7.3	☐	☐
1.4	☐	☐	3.4	☐	☐		5.2	☐	☐				
1.5	☐	☐	3.5	☐	☐		5.2	☐	☐	☐			
			3.6	☐	☐	☐							

* Restart tape *

Stop to read Items 18 - Informal use of language and 32 - Staff-child interactions

Inadequate		Minimal		Good		Excellent
1	2	3	4	5	6	7

18. Informal use of language*

1.1 Staff talk to children primarily to control their behavior and manage routines.

1.2 Staff rarely respond to children's talk.

1.3 Children's talk is discouraged much of the day.

3.1 Some staff-child conversation† (Ex. ask "yes/no" or short answer questions; give short answers to children's questions).

3.2 Children allowed to talk much of the day.

5.1 Many staff-child conversations during free play and routines.

5.2 Language is primarily used by staff to exchange information with children and for social interaction.

5.3 Staff add information to expand‡ on ideas presented by children.**

5.4 Staff encourage communication among children, including those with disabilities (Ex. remind children to listen to one another; teach all children to sign if classmate uses sign language).

7.1 Staff have individual conversations with most of the children.**

7.2 Children are asked questions to encourage them to give longer and more complex answers.** (Ex. young child is asked "what" or "where" questions; older child is asked "why" or "how" questions).

Notes for Clarification

* When multiple staff are working with the children, base the score for this item on the overall impact of the staff's communication with the children. The intent of this item is that children's need for language stimulation is met.

† In order to be given credit for "conversation," there should be some mutual listening and talking/responding from both the staff and child. This is different from one-way communication such as giving directions or commands. For children with less verbal ability, the response may not be in words but may involve gestures, sign language, or communication devices.

‡ Expand means staff respond verbally to add more information to what a child says. For example, a child says, "Look at this truck," and the teacher responds, "It's a red dump truck. See, it has a place to carry things."

** To give credit for these indicators several instances must be observed.

18. Informal use of language 1 2 3 4 5 6 7

	Y	N		Y	N		Y	N		Y	N
1.1	☐	☐	3.1	☐	☐	5.1	☐	☐	7.1	☐	☐
1.2	☐	☐	3.2	☐	☐	5.2	☐	☐	7.2	☐	☐
1.3	☐	☐				5.3	☐	☐			
						5.4	☐	☐			

Inadequate 1	2	Minimal 3	4	Good 5	6	Excellent 7

32. Staff-child interactions*

1.1 Staff members are not responsive to or not involved with children (Ex. ignore children, staff seem distant or cold).

1.2 Interactions are unpleasant (Ex. voices sound strained and irritable).

1.3 Physical contact used principally for control (Ex. hurrying children along) or inappropriately (Ex. unwanted hugs or tickling).

3.1 Staff usually respond to children in a warm, supportive manner (Ex. staff and children seem relaxed, voices cheerful, frequent smiling).

3.2 Few, if any, unpleasant interactions.

5.1 Staff show warmth through appropriate physical contact (Ex. pat child on the back, return child's hug).

5.2 Staff show respect for children (Ex. listen attentively, make eye contact, treat children fairly, do not discriminate).

5.3 Staff respond sympathetically to help children who are upset, hurt, or angry.

7.1 Staff seem to enjoy being with the children.

7.2 Staff encourage the development of mutual respect between children and adults (Ex. staff wait until children finish asking questions before answering; encourage children in a polite way to listen when adults speak).

Note for Clarification

- While the indicators for quality in this item generally hold true across a diversity of cultures and individuals, the ways in which they are expressed may differ. For example, direct eye contact in some cultures is a sign of respect; in others, a sign of disrespect. Similarly, some individuals are more likely to smile and be demonstrative than others. However, the requirements of the indicators must be met, although there can be some variation in the way this is done.

32. Informal use of language 1 2 3 4 5 6 7

	Y	N		Y	N		Y	N		Y	N
1.1	☐	☐	3.1	☐	☐	5.1	☐	☐	7.1	☐	☐
1.2	☐	☐	3.2	☐	☐	5.2	☐	☐	7.2	☐	☐
1.3	☐	☐				5.3	☐	☐			

* Restart tape *

Stop to Score Item 18 - Informed use of language (p. 13) and Item 32 - Staff-child interactions (above)

* Restart tape *

Stop to read Item 7 - Space for gross motor play and Item 8 - Gross motor equipment

Inadequate 1	2	Minimal 3	4	Good 5	6	Excellent 7

7. Space for gross motor play*

Inadequate 1	Minimal 3	Good 5	Excellent 7
1.1 No outdoor or indoor space used for gross motor/physical play. 1.2 Gross motor space is very dangerous (Ex. access requires long walk on busy street; same space used for play and parking lot; unfenced area for preschoolers).	3.1 Some space outdoors or indoors used for gross motor/physical play. 3.2 Gross motor space is generally safe.† (Ex. sufficient cushioning under climbing equipment; fenced in outdoor area).	5.1 Adequate space outdoors and some space indoors.‡ 5.2 Space is easily accessible for children in group (Ex. on same level and near classroom; no barriers for children with disabilities). 5.3 Space is organized so that different types of activities do not interfere with one another (Ex. play with wheel toys separated from climbing equipment and ball play).	7.1 Outdoor gross motor space has a variety of surfaces permitting different types of play (Ex. sand, black top, wood chips; grass). 7.2 Outdoor area has some protection from the elements (Ex. shade in summer, sun in winter, wind break, good drainage). 7.3 Space has convenient features (Ex. close to toilets and drinking water, accessible storage for equipment; class has direct access to outdoors).

Notes for Clarification

* In assessing space for gross motor play, include both outdoor and indoor areas, except where only one is specified in an indicator. All areas regularly available for gross motor play should be considered, even if children are not observed in the area.

† Although no gross motor area that challenges children can ever be completely safe, the intent of this indicator is that the major causes of serious injury are minimized, such as injury from falls, entrapment, pinching of body parts, and protrusions from equipment.

‡ For a rating of 5, space must be adequate for the size of the group using the area. Find out if class groups rotate or if several groups use the space at the same time. Some indoor space must be available for use for gross motor play, especially in bad weather. This space may usually be used for other activities. When required by environmental conditions (ex. extreme weather or pollution; dangerous social conditions), facilities may be given a 5 if they have adequate space indoors and some space outdoors.

Question

(5.1) Is there any indoor space that you use for gross motor play, especially in bad weather?

7. Space for gross motor play 1 2 3 4 5 6 7

	Y	N		Y	N		Y	N		Y	N
1.1	☐	☐	3.1	☐	☐	5.1	☐	☐	7.1	☐	☐
1.2	☐	☐	3.2	☐	☐	5.2	☐	☐	7.2	☐	☐
						5.3	☐	☐	7.3	☐	☐

Inadequate 1	2	Minimal 3	4	Good 5	6	Excellent 7

8. Gross motor equipment*

1.1 Very little gross motor equipment used for play.

1.2 Equipment is generally in poor repair.

1.3 Most of the equipment is not appropriate for the age and ability of the children (Ex. 6-foot tall open slide for preschoolers; adult-sized basketball hoop).

3.1 Some gross motor equipment accessible to all children for at least one hour daily.†

3.2 Equipment is generally in good repair.

3.3 Most of the equipment is appropriate for the age and ability of the children.

5.1 There is enough gross motor equipment so that children have access without a long wait.

5.2 Equipment stimulates a variety of skills (Ex. balancing, climbing, ball play, steering and pedaling wheel toys).

5.3 Adaptations‡ made or special equipment provided for children in group with disabilities. *NA permitted.*

7.1 Both stationary and portable gross motor equipment are used.

7.2 Gross motor equipment stimulates skills on different levels (Ex. tricycles with and without pedals; different sizes of balls; both ramp and ladder access to climbing structure).

Notes for Clarification

* Examples of gross motor equipment: ***stationary equipment*** such as swings, slides, climbing equipment, overhead ladders; ***portable equipment*** such as balls and sports equipment, wheel toys, tumbling mats, jump ropes, bean bags, and ring toss game. When rating gross motor equipment, consider equipment both indoors and outdoors.

† For programs of 4 hours or less, at least half an hour of access is required.

‡ Adaptations include physical modifications to existing equipment or specially designed equipment as well as help from staff to enable children with disabilities to have gross motor experiences similar to those of their peers. Score NA if no children requiring adaptations are enrolled in the group being observed.

8. Gross motor equipment 1 2 3 4 5 6 7

	Y	N		Y	N		Y	N	NA		Y	N
1.1	☐	☐	3.1	☐	☐	5.1	☐	☐		7.1	☐	☐
1.2	☐	☐	3.2	☐	☐	5.2	☐	☐		7.2	☐	☐
1.3	☐	☐	3.3	☐	☐	5.3	☐	☐	☐			

* Restart tape *

Stop to score Item 7 - Space for gross motor play (p. 15) and Item 8 - Gross motor equipment (above)

* Restart tape *

Stop to read Item 29 - Supervision of gross motor activities

Inadequate		Minimal		Good		Excellent
1	2	3	4	5	6	7

29. Supervision of gross motor activities

1.1 Inadequate supervision provided in gross motor area to protect children's health and safety (Ex. children left unattended even for short period of time; not enough adults to watch children in area; staff do not pay attention to children).

1.2 Most staff-child interaction is negative (Ex. staff seem angry; punitive and overly controlling atmosphere).

3.1 Supervision is adequate to protect children's health and safety (Ex. enough staff present to watch children in area; staff positioned to see all areas; staff move around as needed; intervene when problem occurs).

3.2 Some positive staff-child interaction (Ex. comfort child who is upset or hurt; show appreciation of new skill; pleasant tone of voice).

5.1 Staff act to prevent dangerous situations before they occur (Ex. remove broken toys or other dangers prior to children's use; stop rough play before children get hurt).

5.2 Most staff-child interactions are pleasant and helpful.

5.3 Staff assist children to develop skills needed to use equipment (Ex. help children learn to pump on swing; help child with disabilities use adaptive pedals on tricycle).

7.1 Staff talk with children about ideas related to their play (Ex. bring in concepts such as near-far, fast-slow for younger children; ask children to tell about building project or dramatic play).

7.2 Staff help with resources to enhance play (Ex. help set up obstacle course for tricycles).

7.3 Staff help children develop positive social interactions (Ex. help children to take turns on popular equipment; provide equipment that encourages cooperation such as a two-person rocking boat, walkie-talkie communication devices).

* Restart tape *

Stop to score
Item 29 - Supervision of gross motor activities

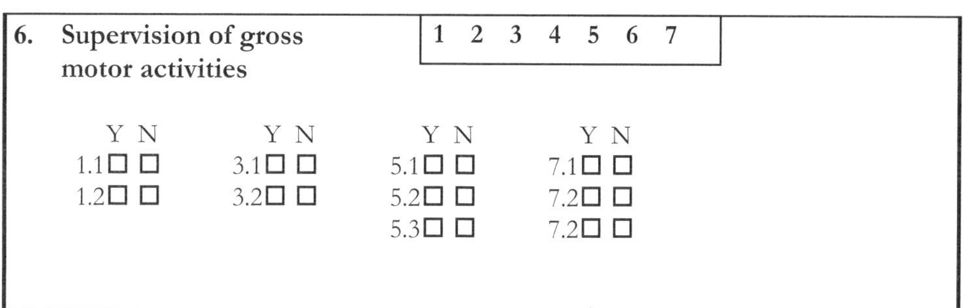

6. Supervision of gross motor activities | 1 2 3 4 5 6 7

Y N	Y N	Y N	Y N
1.1☐ ☐	3.1☐ ☐	5.1☐ ☐	7.1☐ ☐
1.2☐ ☐	3.2☐ ☐	5.2☐ ☐	7.2☐ ☐
		5.3☐ ☐	7.2☐ ☐

* Restart tape *

(Conclusion of Video Observations)

PART III: OPTIONAL ACTIVITIES

A. Asking Questions

When you evaluate another person's group setting, some questions will be necessary since you will not be able to score every item based on what you observe. Since questions can be threatening, the observer needs to counteract any negative effects by asking questions that put as little pressure as possible on the person who is answering yet get the information needed to decide on a score. Care should be taken to avoid leading questions or in any way indicating a preferred response.

During your observation, note on your score sheet the items for which you need to ask questions to determine the quality score. Sample questions are provided in the scale to help you get information to score indicators you could not score based on your observation alone. Feel free to adapt these sample questions, or to ask questions of your own when needed.

Ask questions about one indicator at a time, and take notes or make an immediate decision about the score.

To make the best use of time for questioning, ask questions only when the information is needed to determine the score. If you know from your observation that the room rates at least a 5, then ask questions to get the information to help you decide whether it rates a score of 6 or 7. Don't ask questions needed for a 7 if the room can't rate more than a 3 or 4 based on your observation.

B. Follow-Up Practice Observation

Try using the ECERS-R in a preschool or kindergarten group after you have completed the video training. Plan to observe when the children are active—mornings are usually best. An observation usually takes between 2 to 3 hours. Call ahead to make arrangements with the program. Be sure to explain what you will be doing during the observation, and how much time you will need. Also arrange for a convenient time to ask the teacher some questions, when she is free of caregiving duties with the children.

Before the observation, review the "Instructions for Using the ECERS-R" on pages 5 and 6 of the scale. If possible, observe with a partner who has also completed the video training. Score independently, but observe and ask questions together. After completing the scale, compare and discuss the scores for each item using the ECERS-R *Interrater Reliability* form on pages 19–20. Put your names at the top under "Observers." List your scores for each of the 43 items. First discuss the items on which there is a discrepancy of more than one point. If possible, try to reach consensus on the correct scores. If there is time, go back and discuss any items on which there was not exact agreement. This activity will help you to clarify the reasons for discrepancies. (See the Instructor's Guide for the process by which you can calculate interrater reliability.). Complete several practice observations to increase your competence with the ECERS-R and to feel more at ease with the scale.

TEACHERS COLLEGE PRESS
TEACHERS COLLEGE | COLUMBIA UNIVERSITY
WWW.TCPRESS.COM

ISBN 978-0-8077-3835-1
90000>
9 780807 738351